Evaluating Online Sources

By Ann Truesdell

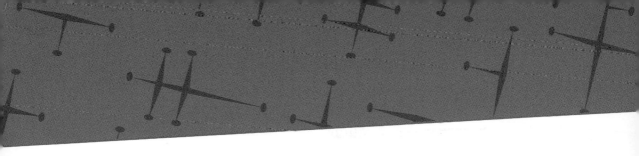

CHERRY LAKE PRESS

Published in the United States of America by Cherry Lake Publishing Group
Ann Arbor, Michigan
www.cherrylakepublishing.com

Series Adviser: Kristin Fontichiaro
Reading Adviser: Marla Conn, MS, Ed., Literacy specialist, Read-Ability, Inc.
Book Designer: Felicia Macheske
Character Illustrator: Rachael McLean

Photo Credits: © ESB Professional/Shutterstock.com, 5; © myboys.me/Shutterstock.com, 7; © Sergey Novikov/Shutterstock.com, 9; © myboys.me/Shutterstock.com, 13; © fizkes/Shutterstock.com, 15; © Naypong Studio/Shutterstock.com, 19

Graphics Credits Throughout: © the simple surface/Shutterstock.com; © Diana Rich/Shutterstock.com; © lemony/Shutterstock.com; © CojoMoxon/Shutterstock.com; © IreneArt/Shutterstock.com; © Artefficient/Shutterstock.com; © Marie Nimrichterova/Shutterstock.com; © Svetolk/Shutterstock.com; © EV-DA/Shutterstock.com; © briddy/Shutterstock.com; © Mix3r/Shutterstock.com

Cherry Lake Press is an imprint of Cherry Lake Publishing Group.

Library of Congress Cataloging-in-Publication Data

Names: Truesdell, Ann, author. | McLean, Rachael, illustrator.
Title: Evaluating online sources / by Ann Truesdell ; illustrated by Rachael McLean.
Description: Ann Arbor, Michigan : Cherry Lake Publishing, 2020. | Series: Create and share : thinking digitally | Includes bibliographical references and index. | Audience: Grades 2-3
Identifiers: LCCN 2020006905 (print) | LCCN 2020006906 (ebook) | ISBN 9781534168688 (hardcover) | ISBN 9781534170360 (paperback) | ISBN 9781534172203 (pdf) | ISBN 9781534174047 (ebook)
Subjects: LCSH: Internet—Safety measures—Juvenile literature. | Internet and children—Juvenile literature.
Classification: LCC TK5105.875.I57 T78 2020 (print) | LCC TK5105.875.I57 (ebook) | DDC 001.40285/4678—dc23
LC record available at https://lccn.loc.gov/2020006905
LC ebook record available at https://lccn.loc.gov/2020006906

Cherry Lake Publishing Group would like to acknowledge the work of the Partnership for 21st Century Learning, a Network of Battelle for Kids. Please visit *http://www.battelleforkids.org/networks/p21* for more information.

Printed in the United States of America
Corporate Graphics

Table of CONTENTS

CHAPTER ONE

Why Evaluate?

Humans are curious creatures. We have lots of questions, and the internet seems to have all of the answers. Unfortunately, not all information online is good information. Did you know that anyone can publish a website? This means that many websites are made by people who are not **experts**. Some of the facts they share might not be **accurate**. Just because it's on the internet does not mean it's true!

Every time you read articles online, you should consider the source of the information. A source is the person, place, or thing that you get your information from. When you look at an online source, ask yourself if it is **credible**. Do you think the source is trustworthy?

Librarians can help you find credible online sources!

It can be tricky to find trustworthy sources online. You must **evaluate** every source. That means you always question what you're reading and decide if you can trust the information. You will need to look closely at the source and maybe even **investigate** further.

Wikipedia is a free and popular online encyclopedia. Anyone can help update the entries. Sometimes the people are experts, but not always. Sometimes there are mistakes, but usually other people notice and fix them. Is Wikipedia a credible source?

Try this:

The first step to finding information you can trust is starting with a search process that you trust. Many smart students begin their research at a school or public library website. Librarians are research experts. They choose online resources with information that is credible. These resources often have better information than free websites found with Google or Bing. Many of these online resources even list the best free websites for each topic! Plus, you can find websites that are made especially for children and students. This makes research much easier and more fun!

What sources can you find on your library website? What are your favorites?

When you research, you might spend a lot of time choosing the best sources. Good sources equal good information! Then you can begin taking notes.

CHAPTER TWO

At First Glance

Evaluating and investigating sources starts with looking at what's in front of you. What is the title of the source? This might be confusing. There are often two "titles" to each page. You will often see the title of the website or **database** near the top of the page. You may also see the title of the article or entry on the website. Both titles can give you clues about the source. The titles will help you decide if the source is **relevant** or not. Is this source going to help you find the information you are looking for? Or is it about a different topic than what you are researching?

Next, smart searchers take a peek at the website's **URL** and **domain** name. The URL is the website's address. It might look messy, but it can give you some important clues about the source. A website's domain is the first part of the URL. It tells you a lot about the website as a whole. The **extension** can give you clues about who owns the website.

A URL is similar to a home address.

How up-to-date does your information need to be? If you are researching the American Revolution of 1776, sources that are a few years old are okay. Are you researching the best smartphone to buy? You'd want to look at a site that has been updated in the past few months, not years! Always check the date of your source to see when it was published and when it was last updated. Old, outdated information is not always credible.

Who is the author of the source? Sometimes the author's name is listed under the title with the date. This is called the **byline**. Other times, the author's name is shown at the bottom of the page. What does the source tell you about the author? Try doing a search for the author's name. See if you can find more information about the author at other sites. If an author isn't named, that can be a clue that the source is not very credible. But this isn't always the case. Credible sources like National Geographic or Pebble Go don't often list an author.

ACTIVITY

Try this:

We can learn a lot about sources from a quick glance. Pretend you are researching the history of cars. In each example below, decide if the source might be good for you to use.

1. A source written by an automotive engineer
2. An article on self-driving cars from May 2010
3. A website about used cars, with five advertisements for used car dealerships on the main page
4. An encyclopedia article from a database called "Cars," with a history section
5. An e-book called *Henry Ford's Assembly Line*
6. A website with the URL www.brianluvsSUVS.net

Answers:

1. Yes. An automobile engineer can be considered an expert on the topic of cars. Keep reading!
2. No. This article is probably outdated.
3. No. This website is probably more about making money or selling something.
4. Yes. Encyclopedia articles are great sources of information.
5. Yes. An e-book about a famous carmaker could be very helpful.
6. No. The URL domain name and extension both show that this website might not be professional or factual.

COMMON URL EXTENSIONS

.edu = education; used by schools and colleges

.gov = government; only for use by branches of the U.S. government

.mil = military; only for use by the U.S. military

.com, .org, and .net = Almost anyone can buy these URL extensions.

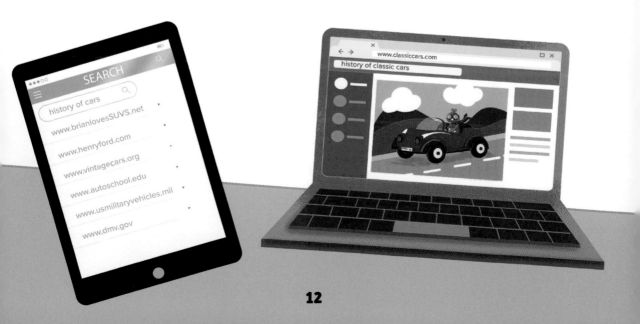

You can learn a lot about a source if you know where to look!

Don't Fall for Fake!

Your investigation might give you some clues about the purpose of the website. Was this source created to inform people? Or does the source want to sell something to people?

Some websites make a lot of money just by having advertisements on the site. Have you visited a page with lots of ads? The website owners get money from each of the companies that have an ad on the page. They often get paid even if you do not click on the ads! These websites try very hard to get you to go to their sites. These sources often have shocking or surprising titles. We call these titles **clickbait**. People are curious, so when they see one of these titles, they might click on it to find out more. Often there is no real information on these sites.

Clickbait titles make people want to learn more.
But these links usually don't lead to any valuable information.

Some sources give inaccurate or wrong information. The internet makes it easy to share information, but this also means it is easy to spread bad information. The tricky thing about inaccurate information is that it is often made to look like real news.

Other information online might be **biased**. Biased information does not give you the whole story. This happens often with elections. A writer who likes the person running for president might only write nice things about that candidate. If they do not like that candidate, they might only write about the bad things the candidate has done. A balanced source would share all the information about a candidate. The article would allow readers to decide for themselves based on the facts.

Voters should research all sides of an issue to get the best information.

ACTIVITY

Try this:

It is important to be able to tell the difference between facts and opinions when you are searching for good sources. This can help you spot bias.

Look at the sentences below about cars. Which statements are facts? Which are opinions? How can you spot the difference?

1. A car is a vehicle that has wheels and a motor.
2. Cars are a better way to travel than planes.
3. Cars allow people to live farther away from their jobs.
4. It is important that Americans buy cars made in Detroit, Michigan.
5. SUVs typically use more gasoline.
6. People should only be allowed to drive electric cars so that we can fix the pollution problem.

Answers:

1. Fact 2. Opinion 3. Fact 4. Opinion 5. Fact 6. Opinion

CHAPTER FOUR

Digging Deeper

Your quick evaluation of a source tells you where to go next. If it does not look like a credible source, you might try and find a new one. But if the source looks pretty good at first glance, your next step is to dig deeper.

If you think you've found a good source, keep the site open. Then open up another tab in your internet browser. Do a quick search for the publication or website title. Try another search for the author's name. What can you find out about the publication, website, or author? Digging deeper by researching the source in other tabs is called lateral reading.

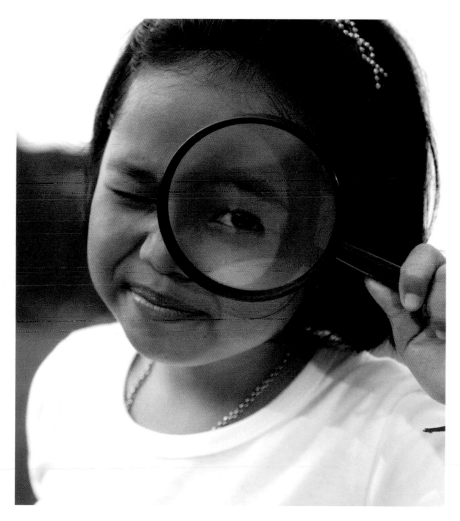

When you find a source that looks pretty good,
open up more tabs to investigate further.

Another important part of lateral reading is fact checking. Open up another tab and see if you can find other sources that state the same facts. Can you find three or more good sources that all share the same fact? If so, this is a good clue that your first source is credible. In fact, many experts recommend that you use at least three different sources to research any serious questions. You will know that you are on the right track when you keep finding the same facts in different sources!

The internet is amazing. It connects us to people and information from all across the world. But it can also lead us to information that is wrong or confusing. The more you practice looking at your sources with an evaluator's eye, the easier your investigations will be!

Try this:

Remember to use your common sense. Does the information make sense? Does it seem odd? Even one or two facts that don't seem quite right can give you clues that the source might not be credible.

Many people have made fake websites to show people how easy it is to make fake information look real. Visit these websites:

- Save the Pacific Northwest Tree Octopus: https://zapatopi. net/treeoctopus
- All About Explorers: https://www.allaboutexplorers.com
- Dog Island: http://www.thedogisland.com

Which ones look the most realistic? What do you see that makes you suspicious of the source? Try visiting fact-checking websites like snopes.com or factcheck.org. What do these websites say about these sources?

GLOSSARY

accurate (AK-yuh-rit) free from mistakes

biased (BYE-uhsd) favoring one person, idea, or point of view more than another, usually unfairly

byline (BYE-line) a line at the beginning of a newspaper or magazine that gives the author's name

clickbait (KLIK-bayt) content, like a title, that is written to make readers want to click it

credible (KRED-uh-buhl) possible to believe

database (DAY-tuh-base) large collection of related information organized and stored in a computer

domain (doh-MAYN) website name

evaluate (ih-VAL-yoo-ate) to judge the value of

experts (EK-spurts) people who know a lot about a certain subject

extension (ik-STEN-shuhn) the ending of a URL, such as ".com" or ".org"

investigate (in-VES-tih-gate) to gather information about something

relevant (REL-uh-vuhnt) important to what is being talked about

URL (YOO AR EL) stands for uniform resource locator; it is the "address" you type into a browser to find a web page

BOOK

Pattison, Darcy. *The Nantucket Sea Monster: A Fake News Story*.
Little Rock, AR: Mims House, 2017.

WEBSITE

YouTube—Writing Videos for Kids: How to Evaluate Sources for Reliability
https://youtu.be/q1k8rcYUmbQ
Watch this informative video about evaluating sources.

INDEX

About the AUTHOR

Ann Truesdell is a school librarian in Michigan. She and her husband, Mike, are the proud parents of James, Charlotte, Matilda, and Alice. They all enjoy reading, traveling, being outside, and spending time with their dog, Leia.